MW01443320

Made in United States
Orlando, FL
22 January 2024

42792791R00065